To my Wolf-Brother
I hope these poems
speak to you like
they do to me -
all my love

Jo

FINDING TRUE NORTH *& Critter*

FINDING TRUE NORTH

& Critter

W. M. Ransom

Certain of these poems have appeared in the following publications: New Mexico Magazine, New York Quarterly, Edge (New Zealand), the goodly co, Spectrum, Ironwood, Quetzal, Inscape, Copperhead, Port Townsend Journal, and Paintbrush.

The NAVIGATIO is reprinted with the permission of Dover Publication, Inc.

Library of Congress Catalog Card Number: 73-92744

ISBN 0-914742-02-7

Printed in the United States of America

Second printing

COPPER CANYON PRESS
Box 271
Port Townsend, Washington 98368

to Kathy and Hali

Contents

FINDING TRUE NORTH

Three Ghazals

FISHING THE YELLOWJACKET

MOVING IN

WATERFRONT CAFE

Critter

FINDING TRUE NORTH

GRANDPA'S .45

Lifting, both hands pulling whitely.
How did Hoppy do it one-handed every Saturday?
Grandpa cocks it: tic tic.
Blinking like a startled lizard
in some green rain cobweb swamp
I squeeze, and shake, and squeeze.

I am deaf, floating on my skinny back
in choking swirls of bark and burnt powder.

"...it it."

I'm up on one elbow, blurring.
Dad's there, by the stump, laughing.
"Be goddamned, he hit it."
And as he points out the neat, off-center hole,
as he laughs the very first laugh I remember him laughing,
I brush my watery eyes, and breathe.

VIEW FROM THE HEARSE

Twisted roots wobble through the park:
old people teetering off benches
fidgeting away these bare seasons.

This quick wind squirms and bumps
up their cotton dresses, baggy pants.
It flutters anxiously around their sleeves
settles, finally, like a homesick cat
against their thin gray skins.

That one's heart sucks slowly,
pale octopus in a tide-pool.
He puckers his cheeks—
yellow cheeks, like a field after haying.

He slides his very black hat to his chest,
shades that octopus, that milk-white hunger
that cold, eight-fingered moon that begs me in.

INDIAN SUMMER: MONTANA, 1956

for Gene Left Hand

Not in my saddle, but above it.
"Even eagles have to land," I thought.
My right cheek twitched down:
leather, blister, bruise, bone.
Up again.
My thighs were tight humming wires.
My uncle's foaming roan muscled smoothly
into your uncle's Appaloosas mare.
I could have been more excited.

After noon we bucked bales
to our own long slow rhythm.
My raw hands made riding in easy.

That night, after burning black ticks
out of our glowing burnt hides,
you kicked the fire down, looked up
and said, "We came from there."
You slept safely in a whirl of stars.
At daybreak I chose a longer, dustier way home.

MESSAGE FROM OHANAPECOSH GLACIER

I have seen the soft light flicker,
seen the nose and fingers pressed flat,
fogging the ice at my feet, sinking.
That is no spirit.
Chants echo white in her deep eyes,
blackening visions shift hourly above her face.
She is never dry.
Put your ear to the ice:
a long, stuttering groan.
She is blue, arthritic, naked.
She hunts a lover.
Leave everything here.
Her trail is this twisting stream
that she sends, milky, to the sea.

ON THE MORNING OF THE THIRD NIGHT ABOVE NISQUALLY

Images drip down my back like sweat.
From this hunger I can see time.
Dreams float in deep green whirls under that fog.
Four brown bears stepped through,
mist washing around them like steam
or old reluctant spirits.
We bowed in a ritual I did not know I knew.
A white woman stumbled slowly past
children bent her long pale back.
Her blue eyes opened like the sun
and two white scars sunk through my chest.
The bears shuffled close, shook their manes
and waved their heavy arms against her.
She dropped the children and they grew like gods.
Bear smell thickened, they backed around me like walls.
She touched the bears and they were stone.
She stacked them down there by the creek,
her children standing guard like pillars
and her breasts hanging golden in the sun.
She lumbers up the hill, low to the ground,
her hot skin wet under mud and matted fur of bear.
Tonight she comes for me.

PUYALLUP RIVER

Visions trip me up.
A clumsy dog snorts in the fog,
pads the bank like a walrus on patrol.

Now she is out of focus,
and I am behind my vision
on a river with no dog.
The trees here are many years shorter.
The gunny sack that I used to carry
swells with a man's weight of traps,
scarred salmon and muskrat hides.
I stand and watch myself—
dull, nearsighted trudge.
I shoulder the sack up there by the bend,
wipe my nose on my crusty sleeve,
slip into the dark at the edge of the trees.

The dog licks my hand and the river runs older.
Tears are stones in this singing water
and a strange swamp-thickness
glows through that soft old river in my bones.

A GIFT POEM

for Ron Lampard

McKenna Creek creeps west shallowly
slowly as a swamp.
The mist rises early, like Bigfoot
and spends the day in secret
somewhere near the coast.
Your line thlips the water.

This land feels your footsteps.
It has felt the footsteps
of all your fathers.

I slip two dried snail shells into my creel
barter for my daughter.
You signal that you're moving on.
I reel in a series of record dreams
and follow.

FROM THE PARK

Ducks remark dryly on the lawn,
snuffle hungrily through damp orange,
musty brown leaves.
Backs to the pond,
they gather on paths
mutter their way up alleys
patter grayly into cold streets, empty lots,
melt so very slowly into the reddening
into the ruffling sun.

NEW MOON

Ant dunes mumble under blue fog.
One bare tree spears the dark—
tall crackle of bones
wet as a black eel
black as earth.

Ant dunes mumble under blue fog.
Black as earth
tipping crumbling crumpling
one long damp tree pushes back mud
melts, becomes mud.

THE AFFAIR

Time time
check-out time
knock like a woodpecker
marking time

Distance between your sheets
lies hot like a coiled dragon.

Liar liar
pants on fire
hang your clothes from a
telephone wire

You sip nothing.
Eyes and love are gulped
scalding your soft throated sighs.

Ring around the Rosey
pocket full of Posey
Ashes Ashes
We all fall down

It's a little like playing doctor
in the bushes behind the coal bin.
This time the dust marks your insides,
your patience trembles.

Cry-Baby Cry-Baby
Nyah Nyah Nyah
Cry for your Mama
Cry for your Pa
Cry for the burn on your
Nyah Nyah Nyah

Mayflies live one day and one night.
They float high: coupling, recoupling
dying on leaves, streams
in quick pink trout-mouths
done in finally by their own crippling love.
Cry, baby, cry.

TO AN UGLY STEPFATHER

(on behalf of my student)

Now she is 16, chunky, and (so she tells me)
One with Christ.
You'd not be interested in her.
She hums clumsy hymns in class
and drops crackled snatches of poems,
a trickle of fresh crumbs,
between her uncarved desk and the door.
She was only three, she writes,
when you showed it to her
and asked if it wasn't really
the biggest one she'd ever seen
and put her shaking fist around it
and moved her on it like a fluttering monkey
and begged her not to tell.

When your dreams
are soft little frightened hands
skipping, skipping
up and down your rosey shaft
be comforted.
She would never hunt you out
in the sweating night
in the crawling moon.

4:10 a.m.

for the Tretheweys

Foghorns in Port Townsend moan back and forth:
humpback whales twisting through thick brown kelp
blue whale calves lost from the herd
narwhales with shattered horns
thrashing a bloody foam in jagged tide-pools
sperm whales mating and wanting to mate
flush with a dark whale-love, a glow,
a secret whale-fever that drags long beneath them
alone, at low tide
cold, in the wrong sea.

CATECHISM, 1958

She hovered hooded, blue-eyed:
"What happens to those souls
who take their own lives?"
Your eyes inspected your desk, hopelessly.
"Stand when called upon!"
Your so-white hands
shook like ginkgo leaves
breathless tears moved you slowly to the door.
I sat, quiet as packed dirt.
"If you leave this room
keep on going."
Years behind those flooded eyes
your father dangled like a burnt moth
from a noose in our old tree house.

Both of us kept on going.

SEATTLE: SUMMER, 1963

A low mouth laps water.
Weeds, weeds how I love you.

—Roethke

He shuffle-steps, scruffy bear
high on tiptoe, rolling slowly,
snuffling trouble
wary victim of treacherous eyes
(winter eyes, upward-inward)
winded remnant of tideless seasons.
He is hounded, scuttles sideways
scurries, becomes bottom
becomes rock.
His breath holds him.
He rises gently and swells
but does not burst.
He casts welcome shadows.
He is hungry and is not eaten.
He is Lot's wife and Thomas à Becket.
He is still.

DOUBLE FEATURE

The mirror creaks open like a loose board.
I lather and stare.
Darkness crouches in sunken eyes.
Not my eyes. My eyes.

I limp into the day,
crippled coyote snarling at shadows,
at musty caves, twisting beasts.

The beasts tap me.
I poke two splayed fingers
into their warm gray jelly.
They shimmer back.

I lather the mirror, the sink:
brush clicking lightly in the mug
and me, relieving the sweating walls
scrawling, "Not me! Not me!"
in foaming soft white drooping swirls.

FINDING TRUE NORTH

for David Wagoner

There are dreams that never stop.
Voices tremble at my shoulder,
spin me around in empty rooms.
I fall into eyes that aren't there,
that echo at me in my rear-view mirror.
I am a road hazard and walk when I can.
My car, knowledgable as a mule,
lurches me into this lush field.
One cow lazes in the far corner.
All the trees with moss on them
cringe beyond the fence.
There's probably a swamp there, to the right,
but it has no frogs.
If the sun moves, it must move West.
My leathered face twists upward
and upward is gone.

Three Ghazals

FISHING THE YELLOWJACKET

A fresh damp snakeskin uncurls,
one last slither wheezes out.

Mountains creak open,
their rumpled backs bank this low fire.

Two gray salamanders scrape and skitter,
playing tag. Or loving. Or hunting.

Even before the first crisp light,
stone flies dapple the water.

We shuck our thick night skins and glide,
prehensile, across the long blue dawn.

MOVING IN

No silence beyond black space
a long, harmonic hum.

The closer stars twitter
ragged bones hang, rattle.

Humped clouds grunt and moan and whistle
great whales crying blue from the deep.

Soft notes of sweat sigh and sing
a low bass hiss brakes, flattens, stops.

These twinkling cells are a forest
burning out in this long night.

WATERFRONT CAFE

for Darrel Martin

The green cedar wind off the islands curls
through this fog like a handful of hill.

Sand fleas rustle under long whips of kelp
and waves lick cracked planks like arrows.

The woman who spills my coffee clunks
through the morning, an unfendered boat at moorage.

She slips off her glasses
the tide pulls her through the window.

The fog pulls her across the islands
pushes a listing gill-netter desperately to sea.

She turns, sighs, dusts her driftwood
folds and stacks her unmatched napkins.

A loose log turns in the surf outside
waiting, like we are waiting.

Critter

I

Of the secret of the Grail,
he commits a great sin and a great wrong
who undertakes to tell the tale
otherwise than as it should run.

—Bleheris

Sat up all night and lugged at the moon.
Grunted. Nothing changed.
Sun rolled up the mountain.
I could tell about
meadowlarks, finches
or dogwood and poplar,
madronas, cedar—
no, it was Orion I waited for.
Orion and the whisper of a lug,
lug-lug, lug-lug
from the deep black ages
past his light.

Shed on the highway at twilight.
Lured and ate a slow raven—
he fluttered, lost his feathers
but did not change, tasted muddy.
Red-bearded man in a van camped nearby.
Had a dog and a newly pregnant wife.
Eyed him across the moonlight.
Even the leaves stopped breathing.
He withered under his beard,
bright eyes filled his face.
"Lug-lug, lug-lug," and the moonlight
pushed itself across the van
and the man, the van, the dog
the newly pregnant wife were gone.
A soft pause.
Stretched out in the clearing
and slept.
Stretched the clearing around my moulting fur,
and slept.

Orion whirled and pulled,
spun himself through clouds,
twisted and rolled
West to mint, to firs,
to grandfather cedars and sea.

Woke before dawn.
Three bone-suckers snuffled my toes,
my crotch, back of my neck.
Coyotes carry ticks in rotten fur,
never die fat.
I draw coyotes like a lump of ripe carrion.
Sighed.
They slid away like gray desert otters.
Night otters.
They would see this place again,
shadow-place, empty.
They would follow a strong scent,
melt West through blue sage and pinion pine.

Critters found a log bridge
from Orion to Wyoming.
Seven crossed.
Bridge slipped, snapped,
spilled critters across light,
across time.
Seven lugged and wept.
Laid up three hundred winters
in dry rock caves,
ate small bats and sour toads.
Watched for signs, slept lightly,
died slowly
one by one.

Watched them weaken.
Watched them cough, spit, shudder.
Watched them watch me,
watch the moon,
watch Orion.
Watched their fur glaze with dust,
watched their eyes glaze with light,
watched them die.
One by one by one.
There are more numbers
than leaves, than stones,
than stars.
Only one is sad.
One terrifies one terrified.
Only one.

Tired Critter lay on a rock.
Ringed by soft fires outside,
rung by soft hymns inside,
Critter prayed for Critter,
slept again, belly up
head on rock.

Rain.
Hard wind, stinging rain.
Storm swept like a fat black hand
down bluffs, down alleys,
snuffed streets, homes, lights.
Spirits moaned,
canyons wept.
Critter slutched a slick wet cliff
and slept.

II

If a man loses anything
and goes back
and looks carefully for it
he will find it.

—Tatanka Yotanka

River sounds.
River and rustling trees.
Looked out on green, green,
river and green.
Two drakes whistled by
like breath from old nostrils.
They turned, turned,
their steady black eyes my eyes.
They dove into sunrise
melting, rippling
down-canyon, downwind.

I am a heap of compost,
a pile of last year's leaves
mulched through desert
blown into mountains
somehow intact.
O Orion! this country
this star has a magic,too.

Couldn't stand.
Brittle bones locked, ached.
Crawled slowly to water.
Rested, drank.
Silver-green leaves vibrating,
twirling by thousands,
by hundreds of thousands around,
all around, all up and down river,
confused, made Critter dizzy.
Crawled back against a mossy bank,
shut bleary eyes, shut flocks of leaves.
Chewed twigs and buds,
smelled damp pine,
roots, river rocks.
Smelled man.

Looked up, careful.
Red-bearded man.
Red-bearded man sat upstream,
watching, chewing grass.
Eyed me across the clearing.
"Picked you up in the desert,
brought you here.
There's water here.
My home is here."
Lugged.
"You'll be all right," he said.
Like he was talking to a child,
talking to a pet.
Told his wife he found a Sasquatch.
Tracked me for months.
Lug.

Ate scraps from his porch,
cowed his dog, avoided his wife.
He walked at dawn, talked quietly,
talked and talked.
She waddled heavy, flat-footed
across the garden, stringy hair
hiding hard mouth, hungry teeth.
Cleared her throat and spat.
Twisted her small pale mouth
at me, and spat.

"You are ugly, ugly."
And she threw stones.
"You are a lump of garbage."
Stones.
"You smell like an outhouse."
More stones.

Ran up the road,
lumbered along the road,
panted and cowered,
hid in a stand of scrub pine.
Hid like a yak
in a low stand of cabbage.

Sunset.
Rheumatic Critter slogged upstream,
river-numb legs,
sun-numb face,
foolish old mind, tired.
Tired old mind saw white,
heard cries, pain.
Stood above the pass
above the long, long
sun-red lake.
Saw blood, saw white.
Tired old mind saw eyes,
frozen eyes,
hungry eyes, empty.
Looked West, across the lake
across the pass.
Looked down.
Tired old mind saw white,
saw blood,
saw men eating men,
saw black.

III

Within the bier was a body,
And without, on the silk,
There lay a sword
Which was broken in the middle.

—Chretien

Critter dreams upside-down.
Critter dreams inside-out,
backwards.
Man floats by,
white,
bound around
wrapped all around in white.
Bumps Critter,
turns once like a cracked leaf
on a still pond,
bumps Critter,
stops.

Tried to move, to turn.
Tried to lug, lug-lug.
Tried to open crusty eyes,
roll,
squirm out of sleep.
Slid deep, deep,

Thick black boots peeling mud
flop like dead chickens,
drop out of sight.
A burned, twisted twig
swells, crawls toward Critter,
cold, sweaty Critter.

Twisted branch sprouts
bright brass buds,
bright smooth barrel,
blood groove,
Nicks Critter's nose,
belly, genitals.
Tickles Critter's thighs, knees,
swollen throbbing feet.
Hovers low above,
cocks,
stands easy.

Seven women in black and red,
seven dark, weeping women
carry corn and strips of cloth,
fish bones, sand, sea shell bracelets,
obsidian knives and dried moss.
Moaning women step slowly, circle the corpse,
chant strange rhythms in high, quivering voices.

Critter smells corn silk
and sweet, bursting kernels.
Hears heavy stalks groan
into each other, scrape,
whistle their high, growing sounds
across the dark.

Critter sees seven women
chanting, swaying, shuffling
a soft circle around, around.
Their feet are the sound
of stunted corn dying in the sun.
Their eyes are the hollow ends
of cracked bones.

Women turn in their dance,
turn slowly, slowly.
Their hands are stretched
their tears are blood
their cheeks are bone
their bones are dust
their dust is fine,
soft and fine,
blows thick around
close around my helpless head.
Critter thrashes, smothers.
Old Critter chokes.
Dust covers Critter lightly,
holds him down, pats him,
smooths his sleep,
soothes and smooths his twisted sleep.

IV

Life is the breath of a buffalo
in the winter time.
It is the little shadow
which runs across the grass
and loses itself in the Sunset.

—Crowfoot

Soft wet cloth cooled my face,
cleaned thick, numb lips,
crusty nose, eyes.
Red-bearded man lifted my head,
gave me water.
"They're hunting you,"
Croaked a lug.
"I covered your tracks.
You'll have to hide."

Looked past him, West.
Saw the black back of the lake
ripple like fur,
ripple like muscle
in a black bear's flank.

"Old One,
what have you seen?"
Like a crippled gelding
downwind from a mare
Critter dreamed, snorted,
dreamed again.
Saw a brown mouse
come out of the South,
follow a twitching nose
through grass, alfalfa, corn husks.
Mouse into leaves, into earth.
Mouse into grass, into earth.
Mouse into moss, into earth.
Brown into green, into earth.
Wide mouse eyes follow
twitching nose,
sleep dreamless sleep.

"Old One,
can you help us?"
Groaned, sat up.
Lugged.
Red-bearded man listened.
Sat quietly, head cocked,
listened.
Critter lugged and lugged,
lugged and wept.
Critter moaned, grunted,
drew in dirt,
arranged twigs and stones.

Red-bearded man stood,
walked around, chewed grass.
"I don't understand."
Lugged.
"I'll lead them away,
give you time."
Lugged.
The sun was up.
Red-bearded man was gone.

Looked backwards, Eastward,
into the sun.
Watched an eagle rise,
swing into the sun, a yellow torch
rising higher, circling above all,
above sun, lake, pass,
above Critter, earth,
above all.

Lugged at the sun.
Grunted. Nothing changed.
Night rolled up the mountain.
It was Orion I waited for.
Orion and the whisper of a lug,
lug-lug, lug-lug
from the deep black ages
past his light.

Saw Orion rise in the North sky
like a one-horned buffalo.
Saw him turn, shake himself.
Saw his white mane scatter
seven sisters like quail.
Saw him paw, snort, hook Andromeda.
Saw him trample stars, clouds, men.
Saw his breath
in the cold Northern night.
Saw the bottoms of his eyes.
Saw white.